Praise for *Distributary*

"What's the sound of a voice wanting to help/but trapped inside the nets of helping? A man who knows loss like he knows rage, a first skin? In *Distributary*, Luke Johnson speaks that voice in thick and throbbing language, in lines where sound drives desire into burning. Between frenzy and a brick wall, we find that '... loss is a crater / where the living reside.' But we also find pleasure, as Johnson washes us in love, even through the bullets of loss—with water rushing over us and through, over us and through—in these stunning, eloquent poems."

—JAN BEATTY, author of *Dragstripping*

"In *Distributary*, Luke Johnson courageously navigates the tumultuous landscapes of generational trauma, grief, and masculinity. Poem by poem, he unearths the past, exploring the weight of familial legacies—especially in the wake of his father's death—against the backdrop of love and hope as he raises a family of his own. Above all, *Distributary* celebrates renewal. Johnson's astonishing language surprises and satiates us, reminding us of life's inevitable joys. *Distributary* is more than a book—it's an experience that lingers long after you've turned the final page."

—ALEXIS SEARS, author of *Out of Order*

"Stark figurative language lends buoyancy to Luke Johnson's *Distributary* where the speaker breaks away from the psychic ax blade and halts the centrifugal force of family trauma. In the heart of the book lies a poetic sequence that goes full Deep Image and strips the world down to its most elemental resonant images. These poems are grounded in the physical world, and when you touch these pages, you will get Earth on your fingers."

—JEFFREY MCDANIEL, author of *Holidays in the Islands of Grief*

"There's something prayer-like in this book of grief and fathers, something holy that smells of the earth in these poems of rage and love. 'Time is made of miniature gears prone to snap or implode' Luke Johnson writes, and these poems are made of those gears, pausing both memory and time, digging toward something timeless and human."

—MATTHEW OLZMANN, author of *Constellation Route*

"*Distributary*, Luke Johnson's luminous new book, makes the argument that pain, anger, and grief, when distilled into artful truth, have the capacity to connect us with our natural, creaturely selves—and with each other. I particularly admire Johnson's portraits of family life. They're so specific and honest, so attuned to everyday experience, they point the reader toward the idea that we're all connected to a common lineage and broader, communal history. It's rare to find a poetry collection that makes you feel more a part of the world than you were before reading it. *Distributary* is one of those books."

—DAVID RODERICK, author of *The Americans*

"*Distributary*, Luke Johnson's haunting, necessary second collection, employs personal memory as a means of preserving some modicum of goodness and innocence in our fallen world. Meditating on inheritance, Johnson contends with what our parents have passed down while praying hard that we avoid similar transmissions to our children. Though he ultimately knows he cannot stem the damage, Johnson endeavors to mitigate the incessant screaming that punctuates our days, hoping to spare future generations some of the hurt and wreckage we, in this generation, have known."

—IAIN HALEY POLLOCK, author of *All the Possible Bodies*

"Luke Johnson's second collection, *Distributary*, asks time to freeze for a moment. And this pausing is not in the name of forgetting past violences that happen to and around the body, but rather an attempt to survive despite them. Johnson walks us through his moments, holds our hand, lets us know we can survive, too. The memories in this collection collapse in on themselves, repeating. We are left spinning in these memories with 'the rotted oak / [he'd] climb inside / to calm on days /when daddy / found his rifle's / acoustics / pleasing . . . '"

—JASON B. CRAWFORD, author of *YEET!*

Praise for Quiver

"'Such beauty as hurts to behold,' wrote Paul Goodman. This magnificent book is like that. There's an almost Greek sense of fatedness in these poems, of the inevitability of blood relations leading one, not just to disaster, but to cruelty and moral pollution. Maybe you didn't grow up in a family like the one in this book. I did, so let me assure you Luke Johnson got it right: the ferocious longing to pour understanding and generosity over their stories, to admit complicity, to intervene retroactively to protect something, to save someone, anyone. To smash beauty against the story again and again, trying to force it to alchemize into something that can be borne. Why should you walk this via crucis with Luke Johnson, as I'm passionately recommending? For some, to affirm a truth that you already know. For others, as the Greeks believed, to learn from tragedy what's required to be human."

—PATRICK DONNELLY

"*Quiver* is a rare creation full of song and scar, authenticity and Old Testament mythology, of emotional complexity and witness. In a world where empathy is under threat of erasure, these poems of prophetic violence and harmful lineages take responsibility for themselves and remind us of our own responsibilities to each other. These poems both define and push against the edges of our shared American experience. At its heart, *Quiver* paints a multifaceted portrait of personal and communal betweenness. These poems choose to celebrate everything they touch. Even their own ghosts. Even that greater truth that always remains just slightly out of reach, that he refuses to stop reaching toward."

—JOHN SIBLEY WILLIAMS

"In *Quiver*, Luke Johnson's unforgettable debut poetry collection, he invokes The Old Testament, its fires, floods, and prophecies—to reckon with 'all the ways a child drowns, like spiders trapped in spit.' These are harrowing poems. Yet, at the heart of Johnson's unsparing gaze lies enormous compassion—for the ghosts that haunt him, for the child self who carried 'scars without witness.' *Quiver* is a work of glorious complexity—brutal, lyrical, shot through with images that stop you in your tracks. But more than that, these poems look deeply at the ways the sins of the father are visited on successive generations and move toward breaking the cycle."

—ELLEN BASS

"*Quiver* is the most visceral, haunting book of poems I have read in years. Johnson reimagines masculinity and is unafraid to unearth its dark elements, as father, son, and witness to the brutality and beauty in and around us. He writes, "Listen: When/I said boys have a storm inside,/this itch that fills our teeth, I/was sharing in secret. I meant/ we have mothers who gift us ghosts,/our heads upon a trigger." This searing debut is a world of its own, built with fearlessness, tenderness, and grace. Take notice. Luke Johnson has arrived."

—LEE HERRICK

"In *Quiver*, Luke Johnson's inventive eye and sonorous voice seek to 'pry the past apart.' These poems pursue an allusive quietude beyond trauma and tragedy as wide-eyed, we witness a bruised boy become a tender father. Johnson's impressive debut collection stares into sorrow, but doesn't leave us to linger there. Instead, we swallow the darkness so we can breathe in the light."

—MATT RASMUSSEN

"In *Quiver*, Luke Johnson's startling first book, the poems are singing when they are stinging, scalding as they serve up something wildly fresh, slap after exquisite slap. These poems show us how vulnerability bleeds, and what it sees when it does. There is no soft peddling this poetry, with its faith, its strife, and such uncommon artistry."

—ELAINE SEXTON

"In *Quiver*—which, implausibly, is his first full volume—Luke Johnson cements his title as the uncontested master of shadow. These unnerving poems are the rustle in a vast and unrelenting dark, they are both salve and injury to the body, they are numbing slap and uneasy solace. The poet trains your eyes upon things you never wished to see—and holds you there, with chilling narrative and fierce lyric, until terror gives way to beauty. Am I saying....? Yes, that's exactly what I'm saying—*Quiver* will change the way you see."

—PATRICIA SMITH

Distributary

Distributary

Luke Johnson

Poems

TRP: THE UNIVERSITY PRESS OF SHSU
HUNTSVILLE, TEXAS 77341

Library of Congress Cataloging-in-Publication Data
Names: Johnson, Luke, 1981- author.
Title: Distributary : poems / Luke Johnson.
Other titles: Distributary (Compilation)
Description: First edition. | Huntsville, Texas : TRP: The University Press of SHSU, [2025]
Identifiers: LCCN 2025005190 (print) | LCCN 2025005191 (ebook) | ISBN 9781680034264 (trade paperback) | ISBN 9781680034271 (ebook)
Subjects: LCSH: Grief--Poetry. | Fatherhood--Poetry. | LCGFT: Poetry.
Classification: LCC PS3610.O36446 D58 2025 (print) | LCC PS3610.O36446 (ebook) | DDC 811/.6--dc23/eng/20250404
LC record available at https://lccn.loc.gov/2025005190
LC ebook record available at https://lccn.loc.gov/2025005191

FIRST EDITION

Cover art by Megan Merchant
Author photo by Luke Johnson

Cover design by Cody Gates, Happenstance Type-O-Rama
Interior design by Maureen Forys, Happenstance Type-O-Rama

Printed and bound in the United States of America
First Edition Copyright: 2025

TRP: The University Press of SHSU
Huntsville, Texas 77341
texasreviewpress.org

For my firstborn.
Through whom all rivers flow.

BOOKS IN THIS SERIES:

Luke Johnson, *Quiver*

Luke Johnson, *Distributary*

Contents

Author's Note

Dear reader,

When I finished my first book *Quiver* in the early months of 2022, I made the poor assumption (poets make the worst forecasters) that the book's speaker was finished. That I had said everything that needed to be said about its world. *Quiver* ends with the shadow father dead and the speaker/reckoner beginning to define his own version of masculinity and life. I am aware what kind of journey that book took you on. I lived it. Every line, phrase, and difficult turn. At times it was daunting, other times so richly rewarding. Right when I felt like the speaker was drowning, he would emerge in a hard-won moment of breath. But why am I telling you this? Because the poems that followed, the poems in this book, felt equally part of *Quiver's* world. Not to say this book cannot stand alone. It can. It champions its own sorrow, delves deeper into time. But for me it feels like a world post-war, when the wreckage riffles in wind and flowers, even the faintest blooms, break the oily, fire-charred surface of the soil. This is not to say this book sings with emerald fields and spring blooms. But I can promise I am taking you there, in some variation, and that the speaker, the same from *Quiver,* is starting to grasp his autonomy, spirit and the goodness of fatherhood. More of this goodness will find its way in the third book of what's become a poetic trilogy. There is a grainy melancholia, a grief both personal and cultural in these pages. A daughter's disease, gun violence, time collapse. But by the book's end, the boy in *Quiver* has begun to burgeon out brighter, more whole. The beauty of loss, its quiet distributaries. How the water continues to move no matter the obstacle. Carves inlets, floodplains, endless estuaries. Carves hope.

Best,
Luke Johnson
1/1/24

America

For you, my love, I swallow
this knife. & if not this knife
a bushel of swallows,
who slap the hood while I pin
the pedal, free hand floating
the smog. But what of pillows
with kept creases,
the shoes left scattered, the socks?
Silent mothers? For you, an apple pie. For you,
the bodies of boys: my body, any
body, anyone. A gown of goat necks
& boat strung with bonnets, a violent sky
violet with rain. Forget me. I too
have tasted spider silk & woven
a home from shrapnel & sea glass, strut
like a muscular god. For you, this foolish weather. The white
noise, the willows, the winnowing fog. For you,
this anguish, its pewter stench. Ten thousand
tongues & the bombs who torched them. For you,
their buried swell.

What I mean when I say water

is my son and I
watch a whale

struggle on the beach
and start to hiss

when air grows thick
and the throng

of its blowhole sputters.
Move on I say *no more*

and my son obeys
with a gaze like Gaza

smoldering. Not a single
bird alive to sing

the living from the shatter.
Only smoke

smoke and glass
and a cello lost

from a second story window,
where a little girl plays

despite her daddy's drinking
and pretends

it a door which sounds
like *adore*,

a dance of echolocation.
I'm worried

if he stares too long
the wounds will smile

and suddenly raptured
under all that awe,

the sandpipers dim
and waves diminish,

leave him clawing
for more. I

read there is a beetle
that eats its husk

and as it burgeons out
a brighter color

collects the shards
and buries it where

a blossom's shriveled
to trick your plane of sight.

And isn't that like a father
afraid of his boy?

The both of them bound
to some kind of ritual

by which I mean shedding,
until all that is left

are lunar lights
and a cry that wafts

like lit spruce over
the day's spent sky.

A little one playing
the cello.

Like Ruin

We could talk about the baby humpback who washed ashore with a belly of trash and the net used for catching thousands of fish. How children circled to see its slick skin flake in the sun of California and the birds, so many of them, glob flesh then raise it back like ruin, one after the other after the other. We could stand around watching the wonder dim as sea diminishes, while parents snap photos and point and crawl into its gaping mouth, to pull out giant teeth. But yesterday, while my daughter danced in a dead field, flowers choked by soot, my son came running with a bullet in his hand and before I had time to take it, stuck it in his mouth and said it tasted like lemons. Kant would argue a seed of violence spreads in silence until, too late, a boy is beckoned to break apart beauty and scatter it. That as it blooms his song diminishes and all chances of goodness are gone. That night I put the bullet in a pocket of mud, and as I planted it heard my son cry, the sting on his tongue: throbbing. Why am I telling you this? I stood before the shell of that beast on that day in July and whispered *sorry* as I told my son *spit*, his mouth flooded with ruin. Imagined its mother a mile off the coast, circling—her panicked calls. Nothing but shadows and shadows.

Witching Stick

All my life
I've listened to clock
hands click

and considered
their carousel
cathartic, even cute,

how time
is made of miniature
gears

prone to snap
or implode.
I threw one once

to watch
it shatter sunlight
in the rose

gold street
and as it spun
was struck

by how the street
is quiet
and the bees a kind

of lavish décor
floating an inch
from the tulips.

I moved among
the world
the way a penny will:

dropped and
discovered, counted
among the lost

and could not clutch
a song
to sway alone with.

Maybe it was
my mother, the way
she flicked

a witching stick
in search
of my dead brother

or my jaundice
sister swallowing
up the stars.

I'd lay around
looking
at antique photos

of familial faces
and find
in their stares

a similar sadness
mirroring
moldy sunflowers.

To pray I turned
the clocks around
and counted

down from ten,
until all there was
were wings of moths

and the buoy
where my mother swam
before grief

became heavy
and her soft falsetto
eaten by rage.

Thirty years,
and I hear the heft
of her

anguished chuff—
door knobs shaken
and slammed.

Tonight I held
my son
while he thrashed

his fists
and wailed because
he too

had dreamt
of beached whales
and fire

and could not quell
their rapid clicks
calling out for waves.

I wanted to save him,
to mute the whales
with quiet whispers,

but I find the flies
most beautiful,
each collective hum,

and dare not tempt
their sudden affections,
nor dismiss

the time or hour.
You see,
I stood before

a giant clock
in a city in South Peru,
and watched

the sunlight bleed
across the steps,
until all there was

were violent spears
slicing
through the trees.

I was unable
to speak,
small against

its magnetic flame.
The living woken
with one great rush

and the others
reaching for help.

What I mean when I say God

is river is womb skin

is the face of my father
a terrified ruin

is both hands on his throat
as an egret lifts

an ember inches from snow.

Malignant

before I bowl him over
bruise him

beat him   beat him
bang his head

against the blacktop
again and again

and yell *god damn it,*
as his skin bursts

and spills across
my palms and fingers,

my white shirt sleeve
and shorts,

I must first challenge
him in the box

and beg him   once
to take a strong

stride and swing
at the split finger, the curve,

the rising fastball
and rage, yes rage,

of a meteor misting
an inch from his face

and spinning
in a vain pirouette,

to mock him,
make him feel small.
⋆

A man who once
made Nolan Ryan grin

as he greeted him
at a tryout, said

can't throw the heat like you,
but watch it

disappear in the dust
like my mother, after booze,

when his belt
became a liberation

that freed his fingers
of hog farms and flies/of fear,

when storm light
rippled Houston fields,

where retired silos
crouched in wait

and hummed
as sharecroppers

rose and thrust
and groaned and thrust

and returned
with hands curved

inward and crippled,
cracked

from pesticides, bleach.

*

I want to say something
of longing here.

How he'd watch the poor
make love in pain

and moan when burn
beget vibration

then whimsied like a ghost.
There began

his body. Touch.
To tempt a woman

out at dark
and tongue apart

her shame.
My mother tells me

he rarely spoke
or made love.

Would walk the house
at witching hours,

as if someone
sang in static silence

and spun for him
while he studied them.

*

The spin, the vapor,
his mouth a wound:

the whiff, the strike,
fuck you. My father,

who once dragged
elk home still alive

and skinned
them on the porch

pathetic now.
Six months

from in the grave.

I've been told to write about anything

other than children or birds,
or the way my mother limps
the lilacs & laughs beneath
an oxy haze at stray kits curled
in the shade. True: my father
would not kiss her when drunk,
returned from the bar, far too
fixated on pain. On denial,
how his daddy backhanded prayer
& postured over his sleeping body
to brood his dream: awake. Which according
to her was misery. The static heat
that rises from street, the silences. Spare
needles. Crushed pills grooved to
smokeable rhythms. It was touch, the hips,
his hair on her face and a leftover
grunt. His hands before the low mist
teethed. His hands before their teeth.
Before vodka. Smoothed cues cracked
on quarter cost tables. Late walks.
When she'd watch him stroll the perimeter fence,
listening to Patsy Cline. Passing semis.
The glittering glow of an almond grove
empty. A screech owl's fated call.

Chimera

Tonight, rain drapes
the blue acacia

& the streetlights
shimmer, shroud

the cars in shadows.
My sick, who calls

herself daughter, points
at how

the blossoms curl
then commit themselves

to air. She wants
to know where

the scavengers take them,
& why at night

when her name emerges,
they come so close

she could reach a hand, stroke
their knotted pelt.

Pretend she says,
this is all a dream,

& when we wake
we are bodiless voices, vapors

framed in mist.
We watch *I Love Lucy*.

Take turns singing
Frank Sinatra, then sit

by the window
waiting for fawns,

the little ones lost
from their mothers.

As a boy, my father
wiped dust from a rifle

then slowly
framed a five point

& blew until the birds burst
& the beast lay

still in the reeds. In the reeds,
a womb revealed

a doe unborn,
& my father, lost,

spared me the sight,
before slipping

it into the stream. I confess,
when the beast fell

& baby sank,
I could hear a hum

erupt from water
then sweep

across the fields.
It fell like snow

over flowerless trees
& loomed, large,

like an angelic chill, stalking
the news of the living.

Long before this,
when my mom was small

& her father
had not died from cancer,

she was wrestled
from dream

by invisible force
& found, when waking,

a wounded robin,
flapping against the floor.

She bathed the bird
& fed it.

Gave it drops
of water, a bed, & set

it near a lamp
to warm its wing.

In the morning, yes,
the bird was gone,

but for a single feather,
& my mom

began to weep for hours,
afraid

of what she'd done.
That Fall

her father died
& the birds no longer

shared the news
nor squabbled

the streets for seed.
It was as if everything stopped,

she tells me.
No more music son, no mystery.

Tonight, rain drapes
the blue acacia

& sores surface
my daughter's skin, radiate

into her stomach.
I sprinkle lavender, water,

stutter over a prayer.
Place my palm

upon her body
& beg the beast

to transfer pain
& seed its gales

inside me.

O Mother, The Music: With a Nod to Terrance Hayes

by which I mean
the slap of skin
& grunt
& after the grunt,
the slob
who eats your pecan pie

& praises sister
while she spins
in sequins, spins

& lights electric
as the daylight slips,
is not music, mother,

can't be.
What
is music,

is my
eager hand
along
a hunting knife
& the lightest touch of blade
that cuts so cleanly his beard,
& if not his beard the hair
that whigs his saggy nipples
& makes him look impish, small,
so easily eaten

a hyena
with no mane.

Is the warmth
along the
bone-carved handle
                    & nudge of tip
                    to throbbing throat,

that surges as I squeeze & shake & wrestle rage like *wind in a box*, a cat in its cage,
            the scream of a stillborn prayer.

To the therapist who says it's time to move on

I press my ear to earth to listen to flies cluster.
Cradle crows the neighbor's son shoots & stuff
their throats with thumb tacks. I ripped a phone

once from its cord & dug a hole so deep I
could stand inside it sing to my father in hell.
Last night my lover let out Monk in the autumn air

& walked the woods with naked breasts, her hips
still wide from birth. She let my lips traverse
them tenderly. Slur a line of spit like Morse code

& crown her head in moon flowers. When my
son was born he was soundless. Like a horn in
its red case: soundless. The build before orgasm:

soundless. As a boy I watched dad gut a pig, slide
his hand through its stomach: soundless. That night
he fried the tongue in the hog's fat & slurped its soft

heart: soundless. I've tried so many ways to say
goodbye. Hypnosis, late walks, water, God. Shaped
totems out of broken clocks to coax his twisted shadow.

My mentor tells me lines of lyric are open doors
the dead find pleasure in passing through. But no
matter the door there is always a shovel. & no matter

the shovel there is always a loss. & loss is a crater
where the living reside. Yes—someone has to dig.

Distributary

I found a clock
hidden by a quail egg

& slowly, shaking,
lifted it toward light,

to see its insides shift
like underwater smoke.

But before I could
my father's rifle

shattered silence
& sent the swallows

weaving through
a storm cloud.

Perhaps I'm only half
retelling the truth

around the egg
& how the light

was not light
but the brooding dark

that gathered over
homes with chimneys

& erased as it will the trees,
& if not the trees

the creek that gave us
koi to catch if one

was willing to surface.
So few that if I swam

its depths I'd catch
a single fin of copper flash

& follow where a culvert
cut the field & spilled

into a graveyard.
I held my father's

hand there once
& gazed into a hole

in the earth. He
was weeping while

he cleaned a gun
& squinted so his sight

could travel the barrel
with a quartered rag

& wipe away residue.
This before the sick

that ate his blood &
turned him to a shadow.

Before his boy would lift
an egg to look for life

& find inside a single spider
wrapped in human hair.

When he died I watched
my sister curl

into herself & whisper
his name again & again,

as if time could too
be stopped by voice

& the rain reversed,
denial the root of regret.

Divining

When I hit the hog
it ran a mile

through the thicket
and fell

in a foot of water
—drowned.

You hit it in the head
my daddy said,

the zombie effect.
How the body

moves in death
                    a dance

and after
the dance

a knife
that grooves

                                        the bloated gut,
                                                            gropes

like filthy men.
Believe me,

he continues:
even the innocent

eat, son,
throw themselves

in acts
of rage

and reach
for what the world

will offer them.
Later,

the fire
leaps

like magic
from his

fingers and a full
bottle

passed
like prayer.

I pretend to sip.
Spit to ward

the spirit, divination.
A warmth

the body
turns

to torment,
visions. My

daddy in the dark
wood

asking where his
brother is

and why the lake
won't cough him

back.
The babies?

He cut
them clean.

Carbon Pressure

The thing you hate is hidden in the grass. Is groaning. Wants a boy to rub
the urge be urge to suck it first then swallow. Every inch. Is snake in a box
drum, wasp in a jar. Echo, bird feather, breakable rhythm. Art of distance
nearing. You know
no other way to feel.
Your father, a mutt,
the nightjar asleep.
The silence of snow
when the sky caved

in.

Fevered Clove: With a Nod to Brigit Pegeen Kelly

The truth?

There was never
any goat.

Lovers tangled
in the knee

high grass
and groaned

the way
a goat would

when giving birth.
The poet

caught a freckle
of moon

on feral skin
and could taste

the sweat
their teeth exposed,

the spice
of fevered clove.

The song?

Nobody sang.
Unless you

count
the distant cars

on empty
interstates

and sit beside
them turning

the dial,
to scan

for rock n roll.
And then

there is the tongue
that taps

the teeth
and reminds oneself

of Chet Baker.
Or what

about the heart (I
know, the heart,

that useless thing)
that murmurs

like whales
under miles

of water
and makes

of its swell
a heavy explosion?

I want to believe
a head was hung

and as it swayed
the children circled,

pointing to its mouth.
But suppose a poet

watched lovers mingle
and made a music

of the smoke they passed.
The pleasure of touch

like leashing a goat
and leading it into the dark.

Notes on time collapse

I put my ear to my daughter's heart & pray afraid the sick will seize it cause a full

collapse.

A full collapse when mud slides off San Gabriel Mountain & swallows a room of twenty-two children in a seaside church down south.

For months a fox circles her window, leaving behind red lace.

How long before the screaming stops?

As a boy, I witness an egret eats its young, scatter their insides like lace.

I long for mud, its fibrous tendons, to sate on roots that move like fingers, find a pocket of air.

A mother says she can feel them shouting, ghost notes scratching her womb.

Grief, my therapist tells me, *strangles the throat then bloats the body, can cause a psychic split.*

When I pray there are my father's hands, dragging an elk's skinned carcass.

He isn't supposed to marry my prayers, nor slip me from her heart.

This isn't real.

Her heart begins to murmur, sing like whales. We watch a movie on migrating narwhals. How they use the horn to cut through ice & when a calf gets stuck the father spears it, blood like curls of lace.

The story goes there were signs everywhere, fair warning. First the egrets stop laying eggs & then a creek moves backwards. A backwoods preacher calls it *a sign* that *God no longer will grieve.*

On the Sabbath, in high school, I take a wafer & call it His body, slowly sip the blood. Inside me there's a thousand secrets, my body blessed by touch.

Touch is a match that buries the breath, the tongue a witch's refusal.

I refuse to yield to another fever. Spear a hole from a block of ice & rest it on her tongue.

I could be wrong.

My mother warns me to ward the spirits, submit myself to Christ.

I try to be a good son, read my daughter scripture. *Daddy* she says *why would God desire Isaac? What good is causing pain?*

After the egrets stop laying eggs & the creek moves backwards, foxes fill the empty estuary, move like frames of mist.

I confess when I fuck my lover's body, I beg the Lord for grace.

What good is grace without contention, a severing from light?

How long before the screaming stops?

As the baby narwhal bleeds, the mother plunges polar depths,
to spill a pitch that can't be detected, only felt.

My daughter says it starts as a stab than morphs to a shake, radiates into
her bones. *Says Didn't God get it? When Abraham offered Isaac others would follow.*
Even the earth would agree.

At that depth there is no light and pressure obscures sound.

The weight of trees backed by water causes full collapse.

*

The weight of trees backed by water causes full collapse.

At that depth there is no light and pressure obscures sound.

My daughter says it starts as a stab than morphs to a shake, radiates into
her bones. *Says Didn't God get it? When Abraham offered Isaac others would follow.*
Even the earth would agree.

As the baby narwhal bleeds, the mother plunges polar depths,
to spill a pitch that can't be detected, only felt.

How long before the screaming stops?

What good is grace without contention, a severing from light?

I confess when I fuck my lover's body, I beg the Lord for grace.

After the egrets stop laying eggs & the creek moves backwards, foxes fill the empty estuary, move like frames of mist.

I try to be a good son, read my daughter scripture. *Daddy* she says *why would God desire Isaac? What good is causing pain?*

My mother warns me to ward the spirits, submit myself to Christ.

I could be wrong.

I refuse to yield to another fever. Spear a hole from a block of ice & rest it on her tongue.

Touch is a match that buries the breath, the tongue a witch's refusal.

On the sabbath, in high school, I take a wafer & call it His body, slowly sip the blood. Inside me there's a thousand secrets, my body blessed by touch.

The story goes there were signs everywhere, fair warning. First the egrets stop laying eggs & then a creek moves backwards. A backwoods preacher calls it a *sign* that *God no longer will grieve.*

Her heart begins to murmur, sing like whales. We watch a movie on migrating narwhals. How they use the horn to cut through ice & when a calf gets stuck the father spears it, blood like curls of lace.

This isn't real.

He isn't supposed to marry my prayers, nor slip me from her heart.

When I pray there are my father's hands, dragging an elk's skinned carcass.

Grief, my therapist tells me, *strangles the throat then bloats the body, can cause a psychic split.*

A mother says she can feel them shouting, ghost notes scratching her womb.

I long for mud, its fibrous tendons, to sate on roots that move like fingers, find a pocket of air.

As a boy, I witness an egret eats its young, scatter their insides like lace.

How long before the screaming stops?

For months a fox circles her window, leaving behind red lace.

A full collapse when mud slides off San Gabriel Mountain & swallows a room of 22 children in a seaside church down south.

I put my ear to my daughter's heart & pray afraid the sick will seize it, cause a full

collapse.

§

Memory

of the rotted oak
I'd climb inside

to calm on days
when daddy

found his rifle's
acoustics

pleasing,
how I'd fall asleep

to flies vibrations
and wake

at night
to my name

being called—
my mother

flicking a match.

is a pill
my mother lost

in the drain
and her

desperate
for more—

a blue kite
blurred

into yellow.

of a bag of quails
dragged through gravel

and my dad
above them smiling

as he plucked
the feathers

then slit
each belly open

so the heart
could splash

inside a bucket
and darken

as the hours
fell like aphids

from the apple blossoms
and gathered

around my feet.

of my dad
too sick
to stand
on New Year's Eve,
how he
reached
to find
my fingers
and asked,
if ever, I
think of cardinals
thrown
through
a window
in the dark,
a deep whistle
torn
through sky.

of my ear against
the ground
& my mother
above me
begging for answers.
How the nest
began
with a crack
in the concrete
then moved
up the walls,
like fears
in the form
of a question

of my mother
with a sponge
and a bucket
of a bleach.
How she'd
weep
while scrubbing
words
from white tile
my mute
sister scrawled
in crayon
and ask
for a melody,
the pitch
of a bird,
to rise
from my lips
and lead
her out,
into the
radiant snow.

of my nana
rocking
with an afghan
on her lap
and asking
if I see the boy,
the one she lost,
standing
by her bed
and begging
for water,
Sinatra
quietly singing.

of my sister
swinging
both her arms
in summer air
and squeezing
sunlight
like an orange
in her teeth,
the bees
still busy then,
flowers.

of my sister
losing
words
like miniature
combs
and my
mother
behind
her
picking up
pieces.
But never
the right
color
right comb,
always
the wrong
word:
happy instead
of *help*
wither
instead
of *water*,
the *not*
of her
tongue
turned
to *know*.

of the ghostly
croon of Emmylou
while my mom
clipped mint
and pruned bovine
and collected
peas so sweet
I thought
of the fair
and cold coke
and cotton candy
shared between
my sister's
hands and mine,
while we circled
sky in summer
and saw nothing
but blue
nothing but birds,
weaving
their blurred
calligraphy.

of my dad
on the deck

with a blunt
& bottle of rum.

Watch him
bop his

skinny hips
to Patsy Cline

then smile
when he sees

me staring
from my

bedroom window,
a loon

in the foreground
lifting.

of my nana
holding

a single pearl
in lavender light,

then spinning
it over and over,

as if somewhere
inside it

a whisper
is trapped,

the voice
of her stillborn son.

when my
sister was a pig

and the next
a snake,

and no matter
what the pastor

prayed,
would switch

each week
to a new animalia,

and sneak
out into the dark.

of mother
crafting a boat

from mud and feathers
and pushing

it into the stream.

of dad
threshing brush
with a sickle

and the first
spark first snarl,

when smoke
would rise
like twisting

columns
from tinder

and carry his
baritone,
each dumb joke,

over
neighboring oaks

and once,
after his
brother died

of heart disease,
when both of us

wandered
acres deep
for chantarelles

and the chill
in the air a bouquet

of scalpels,
the way he'd reach
then I'd reach back,

the rain
our ritual song.

§

May 24th, 2023

Come close, my love,
& linger under these clouds.

These clouds, cliché, I know,
but sing to them here.

Lay your braid inside
still waters & sing to me here.

So bright a noise the birds refract.
So bright a noise I break, refract.

Refrain from telling me torture, news.
Another school shot,

the slaughter—shoes.
Come dance by the river

in ringlets of rain.
In ringlets of rain

come dance, refrain.
A sharp falsetto I

can't contain.
This rain, this rain, this rain.

May 24th, 2022

Today the birds are gone
  & the grass (can you see it?)
smothers under summer's
  thumb & tumbles toward

the street. Clocks consume
  the hours as my sons
stack cards & scribble in silence—
  daughter under her bed.

She too has heard the gunshots
  dreamt of blood the bodies
of friends' gone rogue with static
  & wonders why when jackals

eat they watch the wounded
  suffer. But what of light
that lingers? Slants against
  the rotted gate & freckles

what the darkness won't,
  a web or muddied mitten.
I boil water. Turn salt & bone
  to broth & soup & slurp

until my shirt's wet. My
  lover's quiet with her
breasts exposed & covered
  in the news. She tells me

of a woman who hopped
    a fence to pull her babies
through an open window
    of a father smashed

into the ground despite his
    daughter's calls. So I play
Leanord Warren. Pace the yard.
    Pray. Sharpen the knives. Imagine

the last note lifted as his heart
    imploded, the Metro stilled
in its sound. Yet maybe it wasn't
    his heart that gave out

but the burden of song built
    by sadness, every abject
terror. A scream. One looped
    melody. The head of a horse

& the buzzards who bored
    it. A barely legible tongue.

It has been so hard to write,

let alone breathe. I go
  to work concerned
my son will find
  a phone in a field
while he runs from gun
  fire and forget my
number. Today, my wife
  attended my daughter's
awards ceremony
  and sent a video of her
too afraid to stand,
  the look on her face:
confused. She wakes
  in sweats at night
and screams when bullets
  spill her mouth
like spiders and dissipate
  into the floor.
As a boy I'd watch
  my mother toss
seeds to city streets
  and wait until she'd
arrive home weeping
  for a brother I
never knew, a boy
  not born, his name
a serrated knife,
  before handing her
water and a little
  blue pill, that put her

soundly to sleep.
   By Spring the streets
would flare with copper
   bees arrive and my
mom would walk
   with her hand
outstretched
   as though holding
someone else's.
   And now I hold
onto what is slipping.
   Ask my son to show
me how he hides
   and critique if I hear
breathing. Demand my
   daughter press her
head to my heart
   and hold until
the static stops.
   The swell of our
blood in sync.

Boy Fury

& when
finally I froze

& the deer
who stopped

had started
to sip again,

my son hurtled
the tall grass

& kid you
not, beloved,

leapt like one
in an evening ballet

then bestowed
the quarry a song.

A sound so sweet,
I thought

of my mother
& peaches

& starched sheets
hung

on loosening lines,
that rippled

when storm light
whispered

the cove,
then carried on over

the estuary.
I suppose

I should say
something

of joy here.
How every octave

left his lips,
then rose

like kite string
into trees

to touch
the powdered glow.

Later, after chores,
we'd skip stones,

mom & I,
& maneuver

through the muddy marsh
to basket

tarnished fruit.
All evening

the spoon, wooden,
circling the pot

& mom dusting
pinches of clove

to crack fevered
tannins.

Long before
the roads,

she tells me,
there were roses, native,

planted by no one,
& when

it rained they
frenzied fields,

to feed local deer.
This before

the stories started.
Before lore

turned to legend
& the bushes burned

to make room
for interstate.

Even the smoke
was sweet,

which siphoned
the deer,

leading them out
for clear shot,

for a single chance
at taking one down.

Which is why,
when my son asks

for a plastic gun,
I show him

a monarch
or stream,

a hollowed trunk
he can climb into

& wear
like a wild corset.

I want his hands
to know nothing

of pain,
of quietude caused

by fury.
Of the loon who calls

for a lover
but finds none,

the loon
who calls for a lover.

Olivia Rodrigo, Van Gogh, This Viscous Light

Today, while my daughter sang of damaged hearts
    & son lay curled in the backseat, a sunbird swerved
        through spindled light & splattered on the hood.
            My son began to scream. & as he screamed
        my daughter hummed, nodding to the beat.
    Van Gogh believed to hear one breathe
was far more precious than sight. So he carved his ear
    in a birthday box & autographed the back. Reports
        vary of course & the gift fades to legend. Lovers
            claim she strung the ear to an almond tree
        & watched it sway with snow, others
    that it was wrapped in twine & buried by his grave.
When my lover writhed, I hid my gaze, afraid to watch
    her crown. Her lips blue & body limp, cord a pulsing
        noose. Until a single slap released a howl that calmed
            when latched to suckle. I swear, world, the problem
        is rage, we fear too often *I love you.* The buzz
    in our ears a buzzsaw of fates, swarming for release.
My son had seen the impact, its breaking shoulder
    & begged to leave the dream. I longed to leave it too.
        In days, my daughter would bleed & cripple, crawl
            into the quiet. Not even the trees would stir.
                Not even the birds.

Rupture

My daughter
spins and spins

and never stops
spinning

stops spinning.
The sky

she says,
an artist's scalpel

slicing light
to slivers and shreds.

So much that when
she stops

she slaps the earth
and the bees

ringlet her braid.
Believe me

she says,
inside me

there's a hole
that sucks

the nectar
from my bones

and I cripple.
She shows

me sequins
of slug shit

ant holes
empty bodies

of beetles
the beauty of wind.

How
the beech grass

bends
and shimmers,

shadows
half her face.

We suck cherries
spit seeds

point at planes
that pass

and pretend
each passing

a rupture of fate
to live

in someone else.
Who are you

I whisper
and she says

nobody.
She'd rather

be a ring
on a widow's hand,

a ruby reflecting
the rain.

Or the rain.
Or the vastness of it.

Tether

I was sixteen
when I pressed
the trigger
of an air soft
and felt it
thrust forward.
And felt it
winnow when
the blue jay
plummeted
forty feet
from pine
and started
flipping
like sparks
from a live
M-80. A burst
that blew
the thumb
from the neighbor's
nephew
and later
left
him unable
to write
or hold his
lover's
hand.
It's true before
I wept

I held
the bird
and examined
where
the pellet
entered,
but I refuse
to own the lie
that boys
find pleasure
in breaking things.
Believe me,
for days I
kept the bird
in a sealed
wood box
and before I
could bury it
begged it to wake,
to re-seed song
in its throat.
Thrilled,
my son leads me
through the zoo
and points
to where piranha eat,
the heads
of feeders floating.
Fact: every year
in Argentina
three boys
fall in infested waters,
are stripped

while trying
to swim.
Fact: 90%
of amputees
still feel their
severed limb.
Sometimes we lose
what's most
important to us
and fill it in
with phantoms.
Scientists call
it muscle memory,
the mind re-mapping
neurons.
But what do we
make of those
we've lost
blurring in the rain?
When my father
died I smelled his cigars
could hear him
clear his throat.
If I play his
favorite hit
he speaks in parable,
proposes
hide and seek.
I'm avoiding
where I planted
the bird, friend,
I'm too afraid
to tell you.

So instead
let's watch
the feeders swarm
and awe at how
my son smiles
while pointing to a fin.

St. Veronica

"She suffered a great deal under the care of many doctors, yet instead of getting better she grew worse." —Mark 5:26

Once, after hide & seek in the neighboring estuary, where my son pretended himself a shadow & did not speak nor move for forty minutes, a time that caused me tremendous torment, I drew a bath at dusk to calm, & felt a hand shove my face toward water then hold until I could no longer breathe. I had been thinking of dead kids in school & death by drowning, & how a body bloats before the buzzards clean up. My daughter by now was cursed with bleeds & her skin pure as porcelain, though more like colorless clay. When the pain was bad it came in shrieks & once after the final shriek, when she no longer spoke nor responded to her name, blew a window out above me. In truth it was a rock, & my son, afraid of a beating, crept between two thin pines & contorted his body to look like bark. I've never laid a hand upon him. Not once. Not in that way. Though I have laid a hand in prayer & asked my ancestors to instruct him in the way of tenderness, in what Madame Guyon calls *obscure illumination*, one woven by force & ease like wind & blizzard. Like rain, when in a flash a flood snaps pines, converts to powdered ponds. When the hand let go, I gagged for voice & there my daughter stood. She was quiet & shivering & asking for a drink. I never considered if she was who tried to drown me. Not once. I've always thought I slipped between the surface as I started to dream, & before I faded she pulled me out,

the air our constellation.

Sweetheart

The day before my father died
he dreamed of soot

& said the sky was beautiful.
That birds descended one

by one to pick apart his eyes
& as he hollowed light

erupted scattered in the surf.
When I met him by his bed

I felt the presence of rain
& gripped by fear I fell on my face

pleading to be heard.
By then his eyes had fogged

& mouth gaped
& a crackle like a static signal

lifted from his lips.
I once set fire to a field

at dawn & demanded
when the silo blew God

give me back my life.
I'd lived condemned & thirsty

& longed for what the others had
a home of benediction.

But my mother was not well
& the whispers grew

& the winds who chewed
took whole the redwood holy

in their mouths. Until my hands
began to itch for grace

felt peace in charred suspension.
So I pressed my lips

to taste the swell
& sucked until the smolder stopped

& settled in my skin.
& now I curve my hand

to mirror moving water.
All the stones wombed from fracture

& worn into rhythm.
But first you must break.

& after you break
you must broker fire

the absence of song smear
soot upon your feet.

So riddle me this:

there was a boy above

a wounded bird
while walking on the shore.

The shadow of absence
brooded behind him

& a crater opened.
& the crater could not feel.

It spoke one word
& that word was *help*.

But when he took his hand
to smother it, a thousand

sweetpeas swaddled the air
& sunlight bloomed.

& sunlight said *let go*.
I'm asking if the bird

was there to bless the need.
Or if the need condemned

the thing behind him
& if what stood there was me?

After The Funeral

When the winds
had toppled the dollhouse,
had pushed over the oak,
had made of windows
wrecking glass

and called me out
to greet the rain barefoot
to meet the sky nude,
to wash myself
in muddy waters

and will my body
underneath
to touch the muted black—

when I had touched it,
had made my flesh beech grass
an amphibious ghost,

when I had heard my sister
walk the shore
and woo me back
from boulders
and mutinies of leaves, I

stepped from torrents
slick with silt
and waited
for her fragile grip
to take me back toward home.

Beetroot

Here is where an umbilical budded
like a beetroot. Where my drunk daddy
cut the cord crooked, left a piece
like frayed shoestring. If you put an ear to it,
you can hear cellos slip between ribs,
consume me. Now squint as if looking
through a peephole. Notice a moon-shaped
mark marred from a smoke-butt. I found
pleasure there. I let the cat lick it clean.

Doppelgänger

My daughter puts
her face against the creek

and says
when I smile, the me

beneath me smiles back
but is empty—

silence dressing the trees.

Silence dresses trees
in sequins of ash

and scatters
when implosion

comes from God bombs.
Too easy a name I know,

God bombs.
But when a child watches

buzzards pluck eyes
from infants

and cries,
but cannot

hear herself crying,
what else is there

but silence
and the language of it?

LOOK!
my daughter says

and I do:
flames of light

like shrinking doors
turning

        and returning.

I read a man met fate
while bending

the bow of a cello
and that each

plucked note
echoed the valley

and rose in volume
the further it flew.

That at midnight,
as the enemy slept,

the psalm
of his fingers

foraged a wail
and from them:

frozen children.

I want to say
something

of wind or snow
or how

the powdered mist
coats the pond

causing prey
to statue.

How my daughter
traces her face

in a window
and smears

it when her
breath burns.

But I've already
said that before.

So let me
instead say this:

when my daughter
screams

and belly bloats,
she begs

to be carried
to water.

I lift her
like a lamb

and lay her
curled in

the reeds.
She says she hears

the voice
of a ghost

calling from under
its surface.

That when
she reaches

the girl pulls back
and the two

of them
turn into one.

Dagger: With a Nod to Phil Levine

You stand
at the backdoor reading
What Work Is

and want nothing
but rain
and solitude

and the scarlet
flowers falling
like flamed daggers

from the tulip trees,
when your son
comes running naked

in his striped socks
and starts to shake
his skinny ass

toward sky
and yell what sounds
like fuck

over and over fuck
which means duck,
a flock of them,

weaving trees
in fluid formation

and clanging

a sound so terrible
you think of *Wagner,*
the worst music

ever invented,
lifting from
the blown speakers

of your daddy's Buick,
while he weeps
and laughs and bangs

his head against
the glass
until the grieving,

the voice of his brother,
fades inside
the fractured light

and leans into the river,
where you'll float one
day in a funeral suit

and wait for rain to crack
the clouds
and consume your face.

So holy, a moment,

your son has stopped
to study the fear that

floods your eyes
and drapes
his hand in yours.

Says *daddy come*
dance for the ducks
and you do:

one step
two step
three step

—bow.
Four step
five step

—spin.

On the 1st anniversary of my father's death, I

sit with my uncle in the half-dark watching
I Love Lucy
and laugh at how
my uncle sucks a cigarillo slow enough
the smoke ringlets
his nostrils
and rises
so the fan which slices them
is suddenly   holy
and the flannel coat clutched with father's sweat   holy
and the boots
he wore   holy
and the abalone ashtray   holy
and the hog he shot from fifty yards
and hung on the far wall   holy
the warbling lyrics
of night herons   holy
I press the smoke slow in my palm and pant
quietly   holy
cod on the stovetop: sizzling:

ii.

cod on the stovetop: cold
and my uncle out with a bottle of Boone's
in his lap
and an old mutt licking the wound
on his heel.

I am tempted by the oven flame, the gas

and all its hissing,
how a wolf spider huffs
when caught in a snare
and will eat itself alive. I've swallowed the weather

and wear black to mimic sleeted streets
the spray from passing tires,
but sometimes, warm,
on a day in August,
when the wind
has fucked the white acacia
and wild onions finger
the fields, I
am asked again if what's in me is holy
if a crater is holy

if the weather shift holy.

And the song
of my mouth
is unmoored.

Bless the Mouth

that saunters, silk of spit.

Bless the hand
that holds the head
& bobs it back & forth.

Bless the build, the bridge,
the white noise whittled
from the body's blazed tremolo.

Bless the gaze,
slap of skin, spilled wine.

Bless the wine, the bite,
the tang, sticky pleather.

Bless the pleather.

Bless this humid coming-&-going.

To contort a tongue
to the rhythm of rapture,
a rowboat swept in a flood.

Acknowledgments

Thank you to the following journals where these poems first appeared: *Poetry Daily, Poetry Northwest, Cherry Tree, Bellingham Review, Tahoma Poetry Review, Chicago Quarterly Review, Rust and Moth, Northwest Review, The Meadow, Blue Mountain Review, Spillway, Stonecoast Review, Split Rock Review, Action-Spectacle, Pedestal, Birdcoat Quarterly, Atticus Review, Santa Fe Literary Review, Poetry Online, Tusculum Review, One, West Trade Review, Indianapolis Review, The Shore, Ghost City Review, Maudlin House, Beaver Magazine, One Art, Louisiana Literature, Inflectionist Review, Kissing Dynamite, Ballast, Limp Wrist, Sho Poetry Journal, Cultural Daily.*

Shout out to my editor J. Bruce and the team at TRP, for both believing in me and equally building a press I can believe in. Let's keep this train rolling.

Press homies Daniel Lassell, Raye Hendrix, Ryan Vine, Matt Miller, Joshua Robbins, Octavio Quintanilla, Donovan McAbee, J. Scott Brownlee and Gerard Robledo, y'all inspire me.

Clifford Brooks, you a powerhouse and a real one. Truly. Stop being so damn handsome.

Poets Matthew Wimberley, Kimberly Priest and Anna Sandy Elrod, thank you for your editorial eyes on the earlier versions of this book. You helped immensely.

I'm still floored by the blurbs. Thank you, Iain Haley Pollock, Jan Beatty, Matthew Olzmann, David Roderick, Jeffrey McDaniel and Jason B Crawford.

I want to thank Quebec, my roots, and my nana. Thank the West Coast, Central Coast, the oaks of California. Thank the little town of Cayucos, Ca, where surfers, beach bums and ranchers collided. What a special place to grow up.

Shout out to 90's LBC rap, just cause.

To all my readers, what can I say? No words can adequately express my thanks.

Poet-friends I love you, there are too many to name. But I'd be a fool not to mention my brother, Dare Williams, who is in the thick of life and poetry with me on the daily.

My mom, two sisters, I love you. Dad, I love you. Glad we found forgiveness. Just wish it could have happened before death.

My three babies—Giana, Malakai, Micah—you are my everything. Giana, don't ever forget who you are.

Ciara, my love, you are the source.

About the Author

LUKE JOHNSON's first book, *Quiver*, released fall 2023 from TRP. *Quiver* was named a finalist for the California Book Award and finished finalist for prizes such as the Jake Adam York, The Levis and the Vassar Miller Award. Of *Quiver*, Patricia Smith writes: "Luke Johnson cements his title as the uncontested master of shadow." He's the co-author of *A Slow Indwelling*, a call and response project with the poet Megan Merchant (Harbor Editions).You can read more of his work at *Poetry Daily, Kenyon Review*, *Prairie Schooner*, *Narrative*, *Poetry Northwest*, and elsewhere.